WE PONDER: UNSETTLED MINDS

A COLLECTION OF POEMS

BILLIE BIOKU

ARCHWAY PUBLISHING

Archway Publishing books may be ordered through booksellers or by contacting:

Archway Publishing
1663 Liberty Drive
Bloomington, IN 47403
www.archwaypublishing.com
844-669-3957

ISBN: 978-1-6657-4108-8 (sc)
ISBN: 978-1-6657-4109-5 (hc)
ISBN: 978-1-6657-4110-1 (e)

Library of Congress Control Number: 2023905554

Print information available on the last page.

Archway Publishing rev. date: 03/21/2023

To my mother,
who never once stopped believing in me.
Thank you!

TABLE OF CONTENTS

AWAKEN DREAMS

MENTAL COLLISIONS

SURREAL LOVE

SPIRITUAL REMEDIES

COMFORT IN THE HEARTBREAK

NATURE'S QUILT

AWESTRUCK SEARCHES

AWAKEN DREAMS

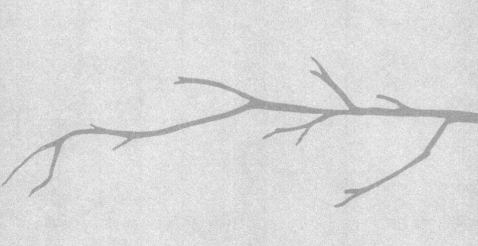

FRIENDS WITHOUT HOMES

Bodies lie down on cold pavements.

Friends without homes sleeping on church pews.

They scare away the churchgoers.

Oh, to be led astray.

The meek shall be blessed, who are you to judge?

Basic necessities always seem to perish.

The hungry man sings in the shallowest of pits.

His clothes torn and shredded with gravy stains.

He lives in a tent that blocks off the sidewalk.

A passerby grows with anger.

She says, "How dare he be present while I walk?"

Feels like the bane of her existence.

I offer a smile to help restore humanities' unwanted.

INQUISITIVE MINDS

Brave souls unfolded by diamond waterfalls.

You're engulfed in the things that cannot be known to man.

Oh, to think so deeply.

We're convinced we have all the right answers, but who are we to kid ourselves?

Developed minds honed by our curiosity.

Like children we are to absorb information as a sponge would.

So, take it all in.

The beauties of the strange and familiar.

The magnitude of grace.

Discovered purposes find the will to live another day.

Delightful knowing that I am not omniscient.

Bountiful mistakes made; we learn of our mistakes.

Joyous dreams still adrift.

ALTITUDES

Hands and feet also have roles to play.

Every intricate detail matters in building up our society.

No job is too insignificant.

Conscious minds show meticulous productivity.

Hardened by the constant judgment.

Feelings shared never told.

The world never falls asleep.

It is always tomorrow somewhere.

We reach the peak with limbs out in the open.

Common trivialities hide out in caves.

They forfeit to the weight of the tides.

All we've known is not all there is to know.

SONDER FEELING

I sit down on a bench and take sips from my London fog latte.

The juxtaposition between hearing chatter from passerby and my silence is overwhelming.

It is peaceful knowing that I do not have to engage.

That I can watch, while being reticent of my emotions.

I think about it every day.

How somehow, we are all interconnected in this world.

All 8 billion of us.

Anywhere I go, I am left with the same thoughts.

People walking, people talking, people breathing.

Like myself, each individual has dreams, a past, and fluttered memories.

Compassionate minds meet kindred spirits.

They, too, could be struggling.

MITOCHONDRIA DEVELOPMENTS

Plans driven by purpose.

My professor once taught that a good leader is one who has a combination of will and humility.

What others say about you determines the type of leader you'll become.

Emotional intelligence lays the foundation of our character.

We should recognize each person's unique gift and work to develop it.

The success of the organization understands the need for diversity.

Everyone's contribution adds to the greater picture.

You cannot fully recover without the help of others.

So, engage in the world with different circumstances.

We work every day to become more selfless.

Calculated net benefits are a strategy to gain experience.

Observation and guidance, we learn from others.

Innovation within the box, problems get solved.

Self-regulation through practiced situations.

Maintained composures, I have the capacity to control.

PHILOSOPHY

The love of wisdom.

Oh, how it makes my heart jump for joy.

My one true love that cannot be taken away.

Metaphysics—the study of reality.

Do humans have souls?

Is the idea of race intrinsic, or merely a social construct?

Why do we remain the same person when one of our parts
is missing?

Epistemology—the theory of knowledge.

How do we know that what we know is the truth?

Do numbers really exist? How did vocabulary come into existence?

Can a sound still be made even if we're not present to hear it?

Ethics—the study of morality.

What makes my moral compass better than the next person?

Do we have an obligation to follow the government?

What is the difference between good and evil?

Join me in the quest of finding the answer to these questions.

COPENHAGEN NIGHTS

Like Henry David Thoreau, I yearn to be in a place of
pure solitude.

Perplexed reactions: I envision neon green stop signs every-
where I go.

The start. The beginning. The commencement.

I want to unlock the Earth's most opulent treasure chest.

Mermaids have found their aquatic home somewhere
in Denmark.

But where do I belong?

Identity politics plays a trick on the mind.

Pollution has no face in the greenest capital of the world.

Greenhouse gases continue to emit at the burning of fossil fuels.

Renewable resources have no stake.

The planet's core has been weakened by our carbon footprint.

Indigenous tribes still face food shortages.

Asthmatic exacerbations.

When will we stop?

MURKY OCCURRENCES

You think you have me all figured out.

But you don't know the real me.

You only know the version I've made you privy to.

I set fire to your vision, relinquishing all the rights I once gave you.

We can no longer be friends.

You're like a leech, sucking me dry every chance you get.

A parasitic symbiosis.

I stayed up 'til 4 am once giving you advice, stupidly neglecting my homework.

That's the type of friend I am.

I pirouette around your tears, helping you to feel better.

But what's the point if you never take my advice?

I'm convinced that you just like to hear yourself speak.

You were my closest friend.

We hung out every single day for a couple of years.

Clearly my life was not my own.

I shake now when I hear the words "best friend."

I could never let someone use me like that again.

DISTANCE UNFOLDS

In the end we are left only with unsolved enigmas.

All I want is peace of mind.

You can take everything away from me, but my thoughts.

I will not tussle.

We dilute our minds to fit in with society.

Contemplated convictions, we come alive.

Reasons we try to figure out.

Neutral findings bring out the nicest things.

New developments, we become the best versions of ourselves.

BECOMING MORE AWARE

Emulsified personas, there's a disparate impact.

We're united by the fact that we are human.

Inexpressible joy, I am kept from tumbling down.

Confidence must be kept together when things seem to be falling apart.

A work in progress, we were promised to be completed.

Those who are weary find their way to gentle hearts.

Take courage, for you are not alone.

Without a framework in hand, you become scattered.

Lost in the details, the plan is forgotten.

Driven purposes, I sometimes feel burn out.

Retrospective to-do lists, I replay the day.

Intuitive formalities, foreigners finally feel at home.

I can feel our paradigm start to shift.

MENTAL COLLISIONS

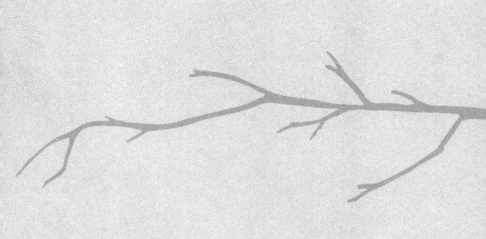

250

Bones wrapped in slices of thick-cut bacon.

Porcelain face mirrors obsolete coffee grounds.

Density remains.

Secreted juices flood the lavatory.

I grow with hunger but crave nothing.

Nutrients deplete from my limp body.

I am weak.

Still, I want to be like Iron Man.

250 calories are all that I can have.

Abductors tear from elliptical descents.

Echoes of reflection parallel my distorted mind.

I was only 17.

LABYRINTH

My mind protects me from the perils of the outside world.

Inside this box I am trapped but alive.

Shouldn't that count for something?

Foreign hands wave caution signs to my neurons.

Filthy boxes compel hand scrubs.

It is never enough.

My fingerprints glaze across the light switch.

Secret touches that no one ever seems to notice.

Three. Five. Seven.

It must always be an odd number.

Trouble lies when I don't oblige.

Unwanted thoughts cloud my brain.

Please make it stop.

Words typed must now be erased.

Eliminate the mistakes. Eliminate the doubts. Eliminate—

Starting over when it doesn't feel right.

Constantly counting consonants and vowels until I am satisfied.

The keys have never left my bag.

Why is this my third time checking?

SPIRALS

My mind is spiraling down.

I'm panic-stricken.

Hands damp with moisture from the saline skin.

My hands try to grab ahold of something sturdy.

Clothes hauled off to reveal a naked body.

I cannot escape.

Flood of heat running down my spine.

Gasping air suffocates my bloodstream.

100 thoughts per minute, I cannot stop.

Disintegrating medicine leaves a bitter taste.

Quiet minds ruminate around passive thoughts.

ICICLES

Sometimes when I cry, I can feel tiny icicles forming on my cheeks.

Why do I cry in the cold?

The icicles start to melt when I enter the shower.

Alpine glaciers bounded by precipitous rock walls.

I can feel the burning hot water melting into my porous skin.

Needles poking turn purple hands.

I don't want it to stop.

Winter has come and I am sad again.

Wrap myself up in a quilted blanket.

I exist to wallow in self-pity.

But, alas I must go.

Why am I sad?

The doctors say it's a chemical imbalance.

Icicles still find a way to formulate on my face.

INSOMNIA

I had hoped to get a good night's rest.

But my mind has decided to jerk from one place to the next.

Replaying the same scenarios from today, I cannot sleep.

Analyzing, deconstructing, critiquing every word that was said.

5 milligrams of Melatonin.

It is now 8 am.

I watched as the Earth tilted on its axis to reveal the sun's glory.

Does the sun ever rise?

A new day has come, and I feel groggy.

I cannot concentrate on my work.

I cannot function.

Oh, if only there were more hours in a day.

All I want to do is catch up on last night's missed rest.

Now I'm left trying to heal this migraine.

INVISIBLE

I am superwoman.

Unbreakable bonds lift the mighty winds.

Take my hand.

Let's run through the wilderness.

Vibrant colors surround the ether.

I cannot find my way through the redwoods.

Fallen logs build a fort.

Rotating bodies form cartwheels around the trees.

Is this what freedom feels like?

Red sockeye salmon relish in the briny saltwater.

But something isn't right.

I am not invincible.

Mortal humans wither away, to dust they return.

Ebbs & Flows fantasize about tranquil summers.

Here comes the solstice slumber.

EUTHYMIC ALCATRAZ

It's like being in a dream, but not realizing that you're in a dream.

I find that each new person I meet brings out a different facet of my personality.

The Assateague wild horses never fail to paint the wind.

I roam freely looking for adventures.

My tears turn to glitter, that's when the fun begins.

I love to make creamy tomato soup with a side of gouda grilled cheese.

Cuba Libre in hand, I'm living the dream.

I rank number one almost every week in Subway Surfers, it helps with the anxiety.

80% of the time I live in my head.

It's kind of cozy here.

Things are going great for me, I can't complain.

Mom, I want you to know that this is what normalcy looks like for me.

I am okay.

BLEAK BOXES

Broken whistles vibrate through the harmonica.

Chopped up time blocks of the air streams.

I exist in a mauve haze.

I count the number of victories and it is not enough.

Sedimentary rocks pile up on top of me.

I do not want to escape.

I've been weathered for too long now.

Exposed to the world to be broken down again.

They try me on like a fedora, abandoning me at the sign of another.

Turn the crank and watch as I burst into flames.

All in the name of jest.

Vacant heart yearns for evanescent souls.

NUZZLED PILLOW

Night has fallen and I am left with my thoughts.

My pillow feels a large thud.

It's the sound of my body collapsing as I enter fetal position.

A sound it knows all too well.

I hope for a peaceful end.

The current washes over me, I do not fight it.

The waves pull me under, I cannot swim.

Garra rufa fish give kisses to my feet.

I can hear the mermaids calling.

Become one of us, they say.

The moonlight caresses my lithe skin.

I am finally free.

But why have I started to float?

Serene eyes engulf my doubts.

This internal battle knows no winner.

HUSHED SECRETS

Emotional obstacles I face, my mind continues to ruminate.

But I haven't reached my optimal peak.

Neurodivergent brain, this is my normal.

Circumstantial triggers, doctors know best.

Preoccupied with the future, there's a level of uncertainty.

Turbulent neutrality, I dig myself into a hole.

Deteriorating brain, chemical compounds come to my rescue.

I take a bath in salty water to enter the repose state.

Unchallenged misconceptions, you don't even try to understand.

I can't open up about what I've been through because society will judge.

They say that they're proponents of mental health but run away at the first sign of illness.

Take a look at what happens if you tell your job.

Silent struggles, I choose wisely who I go to for help.

SURREAL LOVE

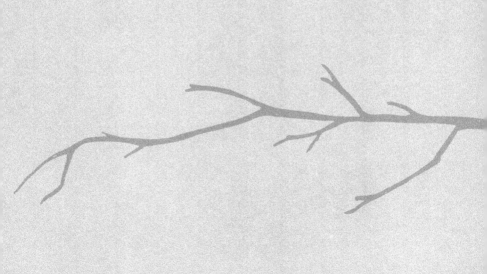

LIMERENCE EFFECT

Our hearts beat through the osmosis persuasion.

Infatuated, I felt as though it was love at first sight.

Perhaps, it was lust at first thought.

Butterflies flutter my mind, caught between the vitamins of the sea.

Hunted down I was the prey you needed.

Gifts of rosemary sourdough and elderflower tea, you spoke to my kneads.

You dowsed my heart with the medicine of devotion.

Craved passions lead to the fondness of the eye.

Massage my mind with soft melodies.

You are what I've been looking for.

NAÏVE EXPLORATIONS

Infinite loops lead the trampoline-goers astray.

Time desires the space in between your compartments.

Mystery tiptoes to the beat of my drum.

I want to know you deeply.

Like narwhals we crave intimacy.

Covered in speculoos I can taste your spice.

Traced fingertips glide on my hips.

Drawn out tiger stripes.

Like a cub you nibble and bite, gnawing on my pulp.

You've memorized the outline of my frame.

Inverted triangle silhouette.

Mesmerized by the glossy brown iris.

Slow adoration rides on tentative invitations.

Sightseeing on the magic of our promises.

EASED COMMITMENTS

My eyes are closed, but my retinas are clear.

A collection of sweet aromatics lies in a little box for when I think of you.

Your cedarwood cologne lingers in my room.

You reek of musk and Banyan fig; I am drawn to you.

Reel me in, tightrope's a fallen.

We continue to write the rulebook of our love story.

Others try to chime in, but we know better than to let them in.

You've been my peace through the heavy storm.

I want to make you feel alright, mollify any pain that may reside.

Wants and desires pleased by the ease of the mind.

Simple lovers' monogamy adores.

COLLISIONS

It's a wavering wandering romance.

We find our way into the desolated room.

Our figures skate around the serene rink.

Thin streams of water stain the eiderdown duvet.

We're caught in a frenzy, this is paradise.

Like wild boars we make guttural sounds.

Submission knows no walls.

Skintight hollow seams.

The tune of euphoria sees blissful awakenings.

BILLIE BIOKU

NASA

I am enthralled with your vibrant soul.

Like an astronaut I find myself gasping for air when you're around.

I explore your space, often enjoying my new findings.

In your space shuttle, we eat about 4 pounds of food a day.

Hmm, I love the taste Of space ice cream.

I sprint across your craters.

We go to your workstation to conduct science experiments.

Quality time well spent; I am satisfied.

Infrared energy transfers through our bodies.

You respond well to the existing atmosphere.

Mass extinctions soon to be near.

High density supernovas create stellar black holes.

You stormed into my world; I couldn't predict your effect.

But, I know that you care deeply for me.

Oh, moon lover, I care for you too.

PHANTOM BEAU

We took a visit to Channel Islands.

I prayed that the water taxi's engine would be our safety net.

A picnic we had while watching gray whales swim in the ocean.

Fig jam, prosciutto, and brie on ciabatta was our delight.

We hiked along the Galápagos, sight-seeing on various types of birds.

I let out an exclamation, pointing fervently at the island scrub-jay.

I turned around to get your attention, but you were gone.

Phantom-like, you only come out at dawn.

I walked past a tree and saw beautiful colored stones on the ground.

Curious, I followed along the path.

There you were.

Down on one knee, you started to recite beautiful poetry.

I was at a complete lost for words.

You asked me if I could love you forever as your life partner.

I said I'd try my best.

There we were, engaged at last.

This time it was real.

You weren't a figment of my imagination.

LOVER'S DELIGHT

Two souls bound by the wreath of love.

Blessed by divine energy, this is holiness.

Set apart for the world to see as a symbol of fidelity.

Eternal proclamations give a glimpse of what's to come.

We communicate through beaming lights of fireflies.

Enamored, I continue to choose you.

Through the trials and tribulations, I am still smitten.

Kind hearts, we are forevermore.

DEAR LOVER,

Remember that time we were in bed listening to
Minnie Riperton?

You adorably struggled to sing along to the "la-la-la" part of her
'Lovin' You' song.

Well, I wanted you to know a few things:

I knew from the start that you were the one I wanted to grow
with in life.

I cherish all the times we drink tea together while
discussing philosophy.

Your gentle kisses adorned by me, you treat me like such a lady.

Sweet soul, you always find a way to care for me even when
you're tired from work.

That's why I try to go above and beyond to make you happy.

I saved all my love for you because I've always been told you
can't hurry good love.

Our hands link through the tungsten hearts.

Your name plus mine engraved in an oak tree out back.

You love me nakedly, flaws and all.

I'm here to stay for the long haul.

VOLCANIC DEPOSITS

We danced around the pleasantries, jellyfish orbit around.

I was already complete when I met you.

Still, you added value to my life.

Lessons I learned from past lovers; I was made wiser.

Is this just another epoch, or are you here to stay?

Calculated fantasies, I hope to know the real you.

We're surrounded by xeric forests.

We sit down and watch alluvium meander through braided channels.

You permeate through my robust walls, twisting and turning through interconnected small openings.

Let's break the surface tension.

You've found the epicenter of my retrograded memory.

Seismic waves start to form from the intensity.

Erupted magma leaves basaltic lava with low viscosity.

Preserved in time we create fossil records.

Aftershocks adjust to the displacement's fissure magnitude.

Zones of seismic gaps remain.

BILLIE BIOKU

VIRTUOUS LOVE

Two grown adults, we work well together.

Constant communication, we don't run away from trouble.

You tell me where I fall short, and I adjust accordingly.

We think about the ways we've might've hurt each other.

We're no strangers to the word "sorry."

Choose your battles wisely; let go of the little things.

Love is a noun; it means you and me.

Though, love is also a verb.

We open the door to the actions of our heart's desires.

Diligent lovers, this was meant to be.

Unconditional, there were never strings attached.

I see the world through your point of view.

It helps me to understand why you act the way you do.

We don't cast blame, but instead engage in self-examination.

I pay attention to the things that you say.

We don't always see eye to eye, but there's constantly an underlying respect.

I accept you as you are, encouraging you to be the best that you can be.

We validate each other's feelings, loving ourselves harder every time.

Thank you for the love letters.

You are my destined loved one.

SPIRITUAL REMEDIES

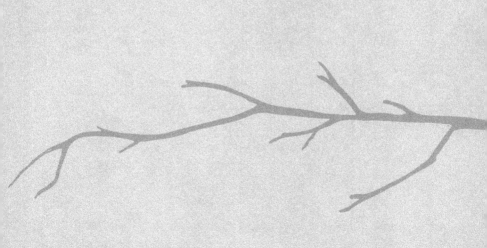

ETHEREAL CREATOR

Your presence beholds the universe.

Like a child, I go to you for milk and honey.

Eternal divinity dances with the elements.

Compositions fuse together to form unusual species.

Narratives we tell, but only You hold the truth.

Anthropomorphic, you transcend the brightest of minds.

Ex Nihilo.

Chaos shapes together to make goodness through order.

Knead my heart, make it pure again.

Animals rule the luminaries.

Have domain over life's creation.

Limited minds and wills chosen to care for Your deepest treasures.

Seeds of doubt planted led to the fall.

Free will given to us, I choose You.

Exquisite One, please forgive us.

SILENT LAMENT

I cry out in pain and agony.

Why me and not them?

But You see everything.

You watch me as I fold into the arms of my lover and let out a large exhale.

This is the third time that I have broken down today.

Roses intertwine with tombstones.

Death illuminates the atmosphere.

Burning sensations fill empty skies.

I cannot see the beauty anymore.

I am hurting, suffering, grieving.

You call me Your masterpiece.

Broken glass welds back together with sharp edges.

I dare not touch.

Scattered days, soul turns numb.

The golden woes of the universe turn to steel.

Living out a continuance with no end in sight.

Better days lie ahead, I think.

MAGENTA COSMOS

Energy that encompasses everything we know.

Spinning wild inhibitions come to a halt.

I let out a blank stare.

Fill up my life with Your pure love.

You found me when I was 18.

I was lost and broken in the depths of my despair.

Made friends with unknown close enemies, who was there
to trust?

Left for dead, my brain was altered.

3 times I knocked on death's door, but You weren't ready for me
to go.

Slowly You were solving my puzzle and making me
whole again.

I often questioned whether You really knew what was best
for me.

But now I know that what I wanted wasn't what I really needed.

Only You know what my heart truly desires.

Though, I wait patiently for a breakthrough.

Implanted in Your love, I've found my home.

Grand designs know no negative spaces.

DECREATION

It was never purely spiritual.

Material possessions decompose into the hickory ground.

Chaos in the midst of glory.

Unhurried measurable death.

Creation unravels as the floodgates of primordial waters open.

Relentless ocean lets out an underwater explosion.

We were warned of the enmity.

Decades of violence, we scream "self-protection."

Humans seek to govern everything.

Human flourishing declines.

I yearn to drink milk and honey from the Creator once again.

Return to nurture and peace.

BROKEN LULLABIES

A child You died to save.

Why must one stay and the other go?

Unveil the truths of the universe to the masses.

Does it hurt to see Your people being mistreated?

Have You forsaken us?

We need Your healing.

Many inquire about Your existence.

Unfathomable concepts are my dessert.

Like children we are made wise again.

Lush fruit hidden beyond Earth's riches.

Intensified energy burns down our souls.

LOST WILLOW

Fragile minds break in the face of adversity.

There was a mirage where I dreamt I could see the unthinkable.

The willow weeps at the sound of Your name.

I walk alone on the moon.

Inconsequential earmarks have receipts end on time.

I vouch for no one.

Rite of passage through the cleansing of bath water.

If you wait patiently, you will find the keys to your good nature.

I will blossom in the dark.

Unstoppable.

I wrestle with the snarling granite gargoyles.

Grotesque figures creep into my dreams.

But I remember that You have always been my North Star.

Seraphim surround me and provide reassurance.

BEWILDERED

I've found the hypotenuse to Your equilibrium.

Unsatisfied minds hold existing evidence at bay.

Overlooked thoughts need no simplification.

Wild hearts roam freely to visualize Your wonders.

I was once buried deep inside.

Spinning around in the gyres of our hemisphere.

Chained doors unlocked at the sound of a roar.

Disgruntled foes run to shelter.

Casted stones leave bruised egos.

My flaws covered with ombre peacocks.

I no longer fear the great unknown.

ADVENT EPIPHANY

Mystified starry eyes loom during the night.

It casts out all doubts and fears.

Fascinated by the beauty produced in all Your works of art.

Extravagant riches flood the ecosystem.

Rivals flee at the sound of Your name.

They don't stand a chance.

I praise Thee with the faintest of hearts.

You've sent the mountain lion to protect me.

Your love feels no resistance from me.

I collapse into Your loving arms, falling apart so gently.

I fawn over You to know You more deeply.

I hand You a list of all my dreams.

You're dreaming them with me.

On this journey learning from place to place.

Gratitude is what I know.

PAVED PERSISTENCY

In the here and now, You have welcomed us.

Our hearts become still from the gush of wind.

Constant reassurances, we are made humble.

At the riverbank, we feel Your presence.

Transient realm, awoken glory.

Our hope lies in the fullness of Your mercy.

Unchangeable, You have the power to change anything at a glide of the fingertips.

Peel back the layers of the never-satisfied world.

We drink from the fountain of parables.

At the end of the day, You are all that we have.

Redeemed love; love redeemed.

PENNED PRAYER

In the essence of my prayer, I am fully known.

Transactions have no hold on the Creator we are made consistently to interact with.

I go to You not only when I'm in trouble, but we also talk throughout the day.

Devoted love, relationships built.

Over a period of time, you answer all of my prayers.

We live in the realm of time and space, but You transcend it.

That is why my prayers sometimes don't get answered instantly.

You take Your time to measure time.

Dark forces fight against Your will, but this is the battleground that we will win.

Advanced strongholds I overcome.

Demolished principalities, I seek Your pleasures.

Perfect execution, lessons learned.

I take delight in You, for our desires are complete.

Spiritual muscles strengthened; I am ready to receive Your answers.

Promises secured, I keep on seeking.

You're shaping our world and curating my destiny.

COMFORT IN THE HEARTBREAK

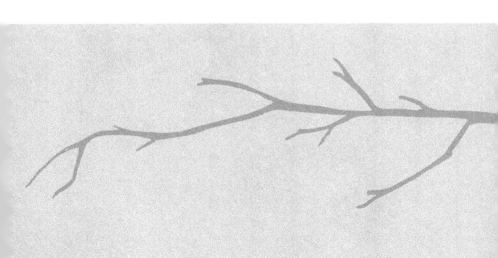

KALEIDOSCOPE

Doomed from the beginning, the glass was half empty.

Signs I pretended I couldn't read.

Eager to be loved and desired.

It cost me a year and some change.

Altered mirrors hid ugly scars.

I was your entertainment.

You made yourself a puppeteer, always believing that you could control my thoughts.

Unread love letters, I felt lost.

Fighting tirelessly to make it work.

Let's be friends.

Left me in the dark to revel with the fine print.

Emotional bounds recognize no title.

Repeated mistakes are a fool's delight.

Warped truths have never been easy to digest.

Perverse actions are no longer welcomed in my home.

POLLUTED LOVE

Shards of pine tree flutter my heart.

A twinge effect meets the aorta.

Localized love story in a different dimension.

You crept into my lowest valley.

Exposed bare mind, I let you in.

Vulnerable to the touch, your deception emerged.

My deepest insecurities left tormented by your wrath.

I was left with nothing.

Fragmented pieces glued together with mildew.

Our love rotten by the sound of warning bells.

Blind lights greeted by charisma.

I was in love with the idea of you.

ENTRANCE TO THE EXHIBITION

Who am I to kid myself?

I know deep down that you'll never change.

I was just another mark on your checklist.

You bragged about how many different races you've tried out.

But mine was a first for you.

Fetish prototypes.

You didn't love me, you never did.

You kept me around long enough to play with.

Disposable, I still carry that feeling around.

You objectified me, never seeing me as a person with real feelings.

The only emotion you attributed to me was anger.

Why are you always mad?

Sorry, that's just my face.

No, actually I'm not sorry.

I told you about the way European beauty standards made me feel, you simply said it didn't exist.

Still, I was crazy for you.

Writing this out, I now realize how down bad I was.

But he's nice to me, I tried to convince myself.

Was he really? Think about it.

I rather be alone than with someone who doesn't share the same values as me.

Ignorance cannot be blissful when education is so vital.

TRAPPED FRAGMENTS

The vile serum you gave me didn't last.

Mirrors expanded through the cobwebs of your lies.

Our love was like a dilapidated shipwreck.

It all came tumbling down as the sun started to shimmer.

Tire tracks pressed against my hollow heart.

Four chambers now filled with debris.

I was ruined.

But like an Egyptian phoenix, I rise again.

From the ashes I become afresh.

No longer made accessible to you.

CRUCIBLE DILEMMAS

Glass bubbles encompass coral reefs.

You were my Chérie Amour.

Your glucose swiftly turned into a foul sour tang.

Fables I believed too soon.

Always misunderstood, you never seemed to get me.

I gave you the cold shoulder as a self-defense.

Every minute you asked if I was angry at you.

Yes, I was angry that you couldn't love me the way that I deserved.

Now irate at the sound of your voice.

Our love once filled with fairytales, has promptly become an old tune.

You were the wrong piece to my complicated puzzle.

Like starfish, I return to binary fission.

BROKEN, NOT DAMAGED

You knew from the beginning that I would be an easy target.

Gullible tales left my innocent mind wanting more.

Subsequently, you weaponized my insecurities.

Like bullet fragments, I was left shattered into pieces.

Devasted, I vowed never to love again.

But how could I give you so much power over my life?

I was made to love and be loved.

Misplaced emotions, I took it out on others.

I knew that they didn't deserve my mistreatment.

To continue loving you would've been like submerging myself in pink ivy.

Venomous poison to the touch.

At the end of the day, the only person that will never leave me is me.

CRATERS OF AFFECTION

I spent 13 hours writing you letters.

I hoped one day you'd replicate my love.

Foolishly believing that you were the one for me.

Spirals of affection, I was in love.

I would've uprooted my whole life just to be with you.

I let you use me as your therapist.

Emotional labor diffused; I was wrenched.

Now left alone in a sorrow of my loneliness.

How did you move on so easily?

In another lifetime, I would choose differently.

DETACHMENT

I rarely show my emotions anymore.

They don't deserve it.

Mental gymnastics with no label, what can we do?

Time after time again I put myself out there, but for what?

Genuine connection skipped our interval.

So, I've stopped caring.

I guard my heart with a metamorphic rock.

System overloaded; I soar the cerulean sky.

I drift through the stratus clouds in search for something real.

I desire someone kind, not nice.

Kindness is the good that happens behind closed doors.

I won't give up on this quest of finding love.

My standards remain the same, I refuse to settle for less.

If you truly want me, you will prove it.

I have a lot of love to give but also need to protect my peace.

ALONE, NOT LONELY

I'll be honest, some company would be nice.

But I greatly value my time and not everyone does.

I don't have time for the mind games, please be straightforward with me.

Tell me what you want and stop wasting my time.

Needy hearts resonate with passionate screams.

Numbed pain to forget about unwanted lovers.

Temporary fixes, I easily let go.

Caught in the moment, I had a bad idea.

Don't flatter yourself, everyone is the one to me.

I'm not quite healed yet, so give me some time.

Right now, I need to be alone.

For my own sake and yours as well.

It's okay if you can't wait for me.

I'll keep sipping on my Chai tea.

SELF-DEVELOPMENT ARC

I've started focusing more on myself.

I've discovered a passion for cooking Thai and Italian foods.

Some of my favorites include Pad Thai, Gnocchi, and Pad See Ew.

I love doing yoga and Pilates to ease my mind in the evening time.

Imagine being in a world where you always feel content.

That's what I am working towards.

Comfort in the midst of disorder.

I am learning to become comfortable with the uncomfortable.

Calm composure held; you cannot break me anymore.

I got a new phone number because limited connections are all I need.

I get to choose who I want to be in my life.

Scarce energy, not all will have access to me.

This is what growth looks like.

Cheers to this new chapter of my life.

NATURE'S QUILT

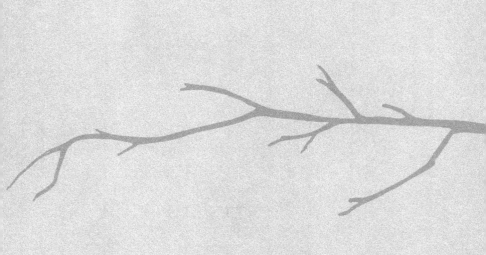

PLACID WATERS

Take me deep into the sea.

Unravel all of who I am.

Cover me with shells and heaps of sand.

I want to see your inner world.

Captivated by the arcane mysteries of the world, I am left wanting more.

Like guppies in a bag, we are stuck.

Treading water, but without fear.

Look at yourself! You radiate beauty and grace like a betta.

Encapsulated by all that we know.

May we never lose our wonder.

LAMBENT LAVENDER

At the snap of a finger comes a glow.

So bright and magnificent it starts to flicker.

It's soft to the touch, leaving my hand feeling transparent.

It gleams and shines like bioluminescent fish in the deep sea.

I see iridescent glitter falling gracefully from the sky.

It forms an indigo hue that instantly helps me to unwind.

You remind me of something woodsy yet sweet.

You surround the fields with your beauty.

It will take me an acre of a year to count all of you.

I want to fall asleep in the evergreen.

SIGHTED STARS

I grow with excitement every time I see you.

You remind me that this Earth is more than meets the eye.

Upon closer inspection I am left feeling dumbfounded.

Swirls of color surround the sky.

Thin air greets the exosphere.

Comets, asteroids, and meteoroids derive from outer space.

Billions of stars enclosed in the Solar System.

Slow movements let out a twinkle in my eye.

RAINY DESERT

Mounds of sand rise above the ground.

It feels like I've been walking for years.

I look around and see nothing but a beige-like brown substance.

Will I ever reach the end?

I do not know how I got here.

I do not know where I am going.

All I know is that I must keep seeking.

I hear a gust of wind coming from the right of me.

I must now run, paradise is near.

Desert pavements kiss sand dunes.

I can feel trickles of something familiar on my face.

I look up in adoration.

Rain.

Oh, how we take the smallest things for granted sometimes.

This desert never sees rain, but today is different.

I grab my canteen to collect the water but notice small holes at the bottom.

I must take what I can get.

I have quenched my thirst.

Onward we go.

PERIWINKLE HYDRANGEA

Take a visit to the garden.

Hydrangea lies ahead.

Hues of pink, blue, white and those in between.

The visual effects of springtime blooms.

Do not be distracted by its beauty.

It carries itself with much tact but is venomous to the touch.

Little children, refrain from taking a bite.

I've heard of its medicinal powers.

Mother, can I have a taste of the candy-colored M&Ms?

They clutter my mind with a blurred effect.

It starts to ooze from my temple.

I drench its essence with water so that it may thrive.

You have given me little to work with.

The wind fails to carry your pollen away.

More and more acid will deepen your blue.

Sepals surround the flower and showcases it to visitors.

One day I will see the periwinkle hydrangea.

NEPTUNE ORBITS

Beauteous blue bulky planet.

165 years to orbit the sallowish sun.

Why so long?

The others wait patiently for you to come around, but it takes light years.

Nails pierce through the atmosphere with a shrill.

Rocks cling onto to the twisted shape-shifting magnetic pull.

Your warmth combusts with the chillness of the ice.

It's like what happens when you put frozen chicken in a hot oily pan.

Explosions.

Maybe it's lonely being in your position.

Dark chilly winds roar out with a stinging sensation.

The moons and rings play hopscotch.

Gravity has no hold on you.

Neptune, please come home.

TREE HANDS

Green cellulose running down your back.

Your hands are rooted in something unknown.

It feels grainy, cold, raw.

Lay down your roots in me.

Together we can build a fortress.

I open your trunk and see you've been here for 100 years.

The circles of life form spirals around your palms.

You are flimsy, I must be careful not to snap your branches off.

Your leaves turn gray when you are sad.

Why are you sad, my friend?

I want to see you produce flowers of your wildest dreams.

Like a genie, you make my wishes come true.

You produce fruit that is so succulent, lush, and sweet.

The hands of labor.

Your hard work will never go unnoticed.

BILLIE BIOKU

HONEYSUCKLE BEE

Sage —

Earthy to the taste.

Rich with jewels of amber.

I consume you when the ocean connects with the sky to let out a drizzle.

I take a teaspoon of you to soothe my throat.

A numbing coziness to the icy arctic.

Wildflower —

Easy to digest, I can finally breathe.

I am invigorated whenever I have a taste of you.

A teaspoon of floral notes wrap around my tongue.

Orange blossom —

A citrus tart flavor exudes from my taste buds.

The sugar particles do gymnastics around the acidity.

Aroma jumps out from the bottle.

The honeybees can't help themselves from having a taste of the nectar.

Clover —
Known by millions, but few really understand you.

You are kind to everyone you meet, never leaving a bitter taste.

You come in three-folds, but where has the lucky one gone

FRACTALS

It's a never-ending loop.

A continuance of distinctive shapes.

Springs and ponds silently watch.

Tremble the affections of the universe.

Forming patterns with our hands, eyes, anything in sight.

The complexity of lines, I am forever in awe.

Frogs jump back-and-forth on a lily pad.

Repetition knows no fault.

Infinite spheres linger until they find a home.

Chaos looms around the simple process.

Below the foam lies the copper ground.

WISPY AIR

Soft clouds form together to make a shape.

Rabbit eyes gaze at me.

Fairy dust sprinkles out from the trees.

Child-like filled with whimsy and nonchalant thoughts.

Skipping fervently with imaginary friends.

Oh, how easy it is to channel my inner child.

She is not done healing. She is not done growing. She is not done being.

Crispy air leaves for apple crumbles.

Blaring music from the boombox of the 90s.

Banana flavored popsicles stains my tongue with a yellow wash.

Roller-skating around the neighborhood, time stops for a while.

Nothing beats water from a hose.

Kids tumble down the hill.

Tag, you're it!

AWESTRUCK SEARCHES

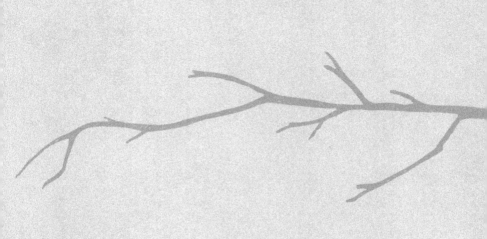

4B, 4C CHIFFON

The sun shines through the mahogany tree dust.

Dust particles settle down on my wooly coiled hair.

Thousands of Z and S-shaped spirals cloak my head.

Kinky corkscrews foresee the garden's play.

Each uniquely picked by the Creator Himself.

Olive oil seeps through my sinuous body.

Whiffs of coconut oil and shea butter.

The darker the berry, the sweeter the nectar.

Melanin squeezed to produce a sap of honey.

Pomegranate liqueur seeds adore.

Cut me open to unravel golden blood.

Streams of water stroke jojoba oil.

Expanding bush in a trance of luscious dreams.

FEATHER PEARL

We search for the mother of pearls in the Pearl of Africa.

It's the mother land.

I came into this world howling and screaming.

Still, no tears were shed.

I've always been that way, resilient.

I punched and kicked as my nana tried to bathe me.

Iya mi you are a fighter; she still says to me.

Fused bones orbit around my skull.

The birth mark on my palm was my kryptonite.

Laughter is what keeps me going.

There's nothing like a mother's love.

Generational trauma binds our hearts together.

A collection of hardships we face.

Don't you dare let them hear you cry.

But I've been strong for too long now.

Soft as a feather, tough as a pearl, we make the perfect balance.

BILLIE BIOKU

TRAVELER'S DEBT

I have seen some of the wonders of the world.

Cascading into to the night, a path has been laid out for me.

Territories transcend invisible borders.

Turtle Island finds its restoration.

Repairing the damage that has been done.

Oh, how so much is owed.

Forced migration left a trail of perpendicular intersections.

Debt still unpaid, we're in a new state of mind.

Mission complete, folks will inquire.

Our ancestor's wildest dreams: inhabitants come alive.

For there are things we can't control.

I heard a whisper saying that we'll be alright.

Still, we scream to be unfettered.

How many times 'til we get it right?

AGILE BLEMISHES

Into the prism I come alive.

Ink blots leave tingles on my toes.

I wander off into the gaping hole.

Run away from the blotches of paint.

I am a canvas.

A glimpse unfolds the unflustered scenery.

Whispers of folk songs play inside of my head.

Magnolia fumes through airtight vents.

Marked up, I am made anew.

BILLIE BIOKU

ADHESION

A dark ash gray illuminates the sky.

Silkworms wrap around the velvet rose.

Sebum oozes from your cerebrum.

I inhale the vaporized molecules as they form.

The populous city overridden by swarms of bees.

Locusts come from down south.

This is the beginning of the end.

Take hold and count your blessings.

GROWTH

Beautiful rose standing alone in the middle of despair.

Take care of a rose, nurture it, and watch as it blossoms.

Deprive it of nutrients and watch it wither away.

Once filled with much vibrancy life, now has lost its way into the unknown.

The sun still shines in the midst of darkness.

The grass bright green, bringing in new creation.

The leaves have fallen, I can hear autumn calling.

Stand still like a stone and take in the beauty of the wilderness.

Are we in a movie?

SUN-KISSED

It's a cool summer day, Sunkist in hand.

I find myself reminiscing on the past.

Many mistakes, ideas, and sunken-cost fallacies.

Why do we continue when all seems to be lost?

The kids; I can hear them gleefully screaming as they frolic in green pastures with ice cream cones in their hands.

When I feel sunken, I think of the kids and the type of message I want to convey to them.

————————————————

All is not lost sweet child.

Stand up, do not sink.

You have been kissed by the sun.

Meant to emit joy into the lives of those around you.

Embrace the sun's warmth, for you are not alone.

BLUE FOX

The blue fox stands by my windowsill at night.

We make eye contact, I break, but she continues.

I can feel her silver eyes piercing through my inner self.

There's a sense of comfort and familiarity. She knows me.

Has she been here before?

She is elegant, kind, and nurturing.

She is stern, spirited, and strong.

I want to be like Sheila the fox, running free in the wilderness.

I can feel the mountain air on my supple skin.

Together we run, far away from our problems and all that
we know.

Morning has come now and there is dew all over me.

I must return home.

Sheila no longer comes by my windowsill.

Farewell, my friend!

BILLIE BIOKU

SWEET POTATOES RECIPE

I pre-heat the oven to 350 degrees Fahrenheit.

I brought home with me 3 Japanese sweet potatoes.

Meticulously, I dice and peel the potatoes.

The baking pan gets dowsed with my choice of Italian olive oil.

The chopped up sweet potatoes get sprinkled with Himalayan salt, rosemary, and cinnamon.

Hmm, I can already smell the aroma.

I pour the mixture onto to the pan, massaging the potatoes into the oil.

Into the oven the large pan goes.

I let the food bake for 45 minutes.

It only comes out once the potatoes are crispy around the edges, but soft and tender to the bite.

I drizzle the top of the sweet potatoes with wildflower honey.

The goodness then gets devoured.

END SCENE

Cayotes coo in grasslands.

Temperate prairies lie in Jackson Hole, Wyoming.

You waltzed right into my life.

We slow dance to Etta James.

I stub my toe on the kitchen island.

You let out a soft chuckle.

We turn back time to our early 20s.

A message in the bottle, our picture goes out to sea.

In our château, I've prepared a charcuterie board.

We watch the dogs play as we drink a glass of Pinot Noir.

Frozen in time, we savor the moment.

CPSIA information can be obtained
at www.ICGtesting.com
Printed in the USA
LVHW041502030423
743330LV00022B/323

9 781665 741088